This 'n' That, Bric a Brac

The Poems of
Barry Plamondon

FriesenPress

Suite 300 - 990 Fort St

Victoria, BC, Canada, V8V 3K2

www.friesenpress.com

ISBN

978-1-4602-7893-2 (Paperback)

978-1-4602-7894-9 (eBook)

1. *Poetry, Canadian*

2. *Poetry, Nature*

3. *Poetry, Family*

Distributed to the trade by The Ingram Book Company

This book is dedicated to my lovely wife Sandi
and my beautiful children
Danielle, Jarred, Dominique, Jakob,
Desirée, Juliette and Darian.
Thanks for your loving support.

Table of Contents

HAIKU 109

FRIENDS AND FAMILY

Peace in Our Home

Peace in our home,
Surely not too much to ask.
Surely we're up to the task,
Peace in our home.

If I Should Stumble

If I should stumble, would you hold me up?
Lend me your arm.
If I should lose my words, would you speak for me?
Keep me from harm.
If I should shiver, would you cover me up?
Keep me warm.
These things I ask,
I hope are not too great a task.
I was strong once, but now I'm not.
Cheated the devil, and I got caught.
I still need people in my life.
Just a few friends and my wife.
Just a few friends and my wife.

Daughters

I am blessed with four daughters.
My life is full of "ums", "ers" and "oughters,"
But when I see one of them smile,
I know then it's all worthwhile.

Sons

Why am I given these three sons, I sometimes ask.
Surely I am not up to the task
Of raising boys to become men.
But when I think about it once again,
It is only then that I see
They are the ones who are raising me.

Dani's Poem

Just a short poem
To say how glad I am you're home.
I'm just not quite the same when you're not here.
My face looks different when I pass by the mirror.
I know you said you had to go away —
You had to climb your mountains and skin
your knees,
Find your heart and ride the breeze.
You said I would never understand,
The time had come to let go your hand.
I am not a smart man nor am I clever.
I do know this though, a father's love is forever.

Father's Day

Again the time of year has come to say
The words we forgot to say when life got
in the way.
Don't think we don't notice the little things
you do,
And all the big ones, too.
As fathers go, you're the best.
You long ago passed that test.
No one could stand above you,
So just a simple note to say
how much we love you.

Darian

A picture of you when you were just small,
Your bushy blond hair and all.
You'll never grow older in your dad's eye.
You'll always just be "My Little Guy."

Friends

Leave no stone unturned when looking for a
friend, for they are hard to find.
Often they come to you, but always they stay
until the end.
They're the one who would give you their all,
Do anything for you no matter how small.
A true friend is something you can never
measure.
When you find one, treat them as if a treasure.
There will always be the fair-weather friends,
the posers, the hangers on,
There is no room in your heart for them — they
don't belong.
A great man once said, "A friend is a gift you
give to yourself."
So here's to friends, I drink to their health.

The Painting

For Juliette, Who Was Sad

You showed me a painting that you'd done.
The others, you said, laughed at it in fun.
I know this was hard for you to understand,
I will always love anything painted by your
tiny hand.
Who is the judge that can honestly say,
They have painted a better work on this day?

What Would You Hear?

What would you hear if you were to
ever listen?
Teardrops fall from little eyes that glisten.
A child struggles to make herself heard.
She knows the answer will be yet another
harsh word.
"Later baby," "Go play," "I'm busy," she's
heard them all.
Still the teardrops fall, still they fall.
What can she do to make her feelings known?
The tree grows as the seed is sown.
God has trusted his children to our care,
To break His trust we do not dare.
Yet many little voices go unheeded,
When a little more love is all that's needed.
What would you hear if you were to ever listen?

The Old Ball Game

Do you remember the game with the ball?
You, and me, and Dani in the hall.
For me that was so much fun
Just to watch you guys laugh and run.
You've gone and grown up now.
Sometimes I can't see how
The time just seemed to slip away so fast.
No matter! I've got enough memories to last.
Today when we meet it's man to man.
That's when I say I love you while I still can.

Always

For Dorene

Don't cry for me, for I am with you still.
I am there in the morning dew on the leaves of
a rose.
I am there on the wind when it blows hard in
the winter.
I am one with the sun and the moon.
I will be with you at every breath you take.
You may not see me, but know this,
I am with you always. Always

Poetry Girl Haiku

The poetry girl,
She is not so big, but wise
Beyond her years.

Higher

At the time of a test a person rises or falls.
Yours was not a fall, but a slip.
You got back up blazing from the hip.
We'll not worry about you, our son.
The world is yours, waiting to be won.
It's in your eyes, the strength, the fire.
You'll only ever climb one way —
That is higher.

One and One Equals Eight

One and one equals eight
"Wrong," you say, but wait!!
Once a young man and woman were wed
"What a beautiful life they'll have," everyone said.
But things were not quite so well, it seems.
For dear old Granny had had many dreams.
In her dreams she had seen grandkids everywhere.
"Just one," she pleaded, "To hold in my rocking
chair."
The young couple were getting no rest.
"Please Granny," they said, "We're doing our best.
But doing their best was not enough
Having that grandchild was going to be tough.
Then one day Granny fell ill with no cure.
Said the couple, "We know what'll fix her for sure."
Sure enough, a few months later a daughter was
born.
It was a snowy winter's morn.
Upon hearing the news, Granny jumped from her
bed with joy.
"Surely," she cried, "Next you'll be having a boy."

It was as if a switch had been turned,
On making babies the young couple had learned.
Next came a boy, then a girl, then a boy,
Until soon enough there were eight.
Now Granny's content to mind the children
While the young couple go to a movie now
and then.
Now I hope you'll believe me,
One and one makes eight.
I must be on my way though, the girls have soccer,
The boys have ball, and I can't be late.

Dominique's Hair

Dominique's hair falls in ringlets to her
shoulder.
Somehow she looks much older.
But I like her just the way she is...as a kid.
I pray she won't make the same mistakes some
of us did.
We all know she'll be grown up soon enough,
And sometimes that can be a little tough.

GARDENS

Seeds

The seeds we planted now have germinated.
It seems so long that we waited.
Tiny green leaves hold the promise of colours
yet to come —
I fear we know not what we've done.
Will nasturtiums and marigolds really go
together?
Will these plants tolerate our weather?
I know it's true — it's best not to fret —
Every seed planted is a treasure not seen yet.

A Cherry Bloomed Today

A cherry bloomed in White Rock today,
A little earlier than usual I'd say.
People stopped to stand and gaze.
The perfect blossoms did amaze,
A sign that spring was knocking at the door —
Please Lord please send us just a few more.

Crocuses

Oh crocus, harbinger of spring,
I love the optimism you bring.
Purples, whites and yellows,
You seem such happy little fellows.
As you set the stage for flowers yet to come,
I'd like to thank you if I may
For a job well done.

The Winter Garden

In the winter garden a witch hazel bloomed.
The summer annuals were long since doomed.
A few winter pansies tried bravely to make a
show,
With blooms of orange, blue or yellow.
Some purple hellebores stood tall in the cold,
While a pink Viburnum proved once again it
was not too cold.
The Cotoneaster and Callicarpa had left their
berries on for show.
I loved this little garden I had come to know.
A prayer of thanks and I was on my way,
The winter garden had made
mine a brighter day.

Ode to a Garden Gnome

There you lay in the garden shattered,
It really should not have mattered.
You were only a garden gnome,
But for years you had made my garden your
home.
You were the guardian of my garden,
A friend: You made me laugh now and then,
With your red peaked cap and little white beard.
Yeah, I know this all sounds a little weird.
When I couldn't find a friend you were there,
With your blank, stupid little stare.
I even tried to glue you back together, to no
avail.
Now I'm off to Walmart to see if
they have gnomes on sale.

Cherry Blossom Snowflakes

Cherry blossom snowflakes fell from the sky.
A spring breeze had just passed us by.
Not a cloud in the sky,
There was a tear in your eye.

The Garden's Mystery

How do you describe a garden? I may never
want to,
For it is the mystery that enchants me, that
lures me
To explore with my eyes, my nose, my touch,
To wonder what lies around the next bend,
To restore the peace that is missing in my soul.
I, for one, enjoy the mystery that is the garden.

The Moonlight, the Roses and You

We stroll tonight in the moonlight garden,
Two lovers in their own perfect Eden.
Shadows dance among the trees and the pale
white blooms of the garden
Give off a ghostly glow.
We are not alone here, I know.
Down through a small glen to the other side,
Here lies the Rose Garden, the owner's pride.
A small bench offers a perfect place to sit and
drink in the garden's scent,
To see the flowers in the moonlight as they
were meant.
I stop to ponder a star, wonder why things are
as they are.
But I don't ponder too long,
Soon we are gone.
Rich men may have gold,
Others thrive on fame, I am told.
But I've done better than anyone could hope to
ever do,
For I have the moonlight, the roses and you.

Angels Among the Roses

I walk the garden in the morn.
It helps me plan my day.
Often my best plans here are born,
If only I could forever stay.
Others may laugh, turn up their noses,
But I know there are angels among the roses.

Mr. Crow

Mr. Crow, you sit on the pole and
complain all day.
I wish that you would just go away.
I've heard all your stories before,
You really are a terrible bore.
I even wish that it might rain,
If that would make you go away again.
Consideration for others is obviously something
you lack,
I just want my peaceful garden back.

Snowdrops

Snowdrops please come out to play,
I long to see you on this cold spring day.
You are a harbinger of better days to come.
I await the cherries, the daffs, the sun.

Neighbours

I had the little old lady across the way
over for tea
In my garden, just her and just me.
She sure had a lot to say,
I could have mistaken her for a squawking jay.
"Your dahlias are too small."
"Have you forgotten the petunias? You have
none at all."
"Tsk, tsk, you really should deadhead more."
"And your toolshed is such an eyesore."
None too soon she left for another date.
I sat alone resigned to my fate.
My ears were ringing with the echoes
of her requests,
And so another lesson learned:
In the garden, caterpillars and
aphids are not the only pests.

A Pot of Sunshine

I keep a pot of sunshine outside my door.
I find it brightens the day so much more.
Those little marigolds have done their share
To brighten many a corner dingy and bare.
They're handy in the border, too.
Many are the things that they can do.
They attract the butterflies.
They're a plant the nematodes despise.
For me I could ask no more
Than to keep them in a pot by my door.

A Garden Stroll

Lovers in the garden stroll
Hand in hand towards the knoll.
There, in tender bliss,
They enjoy a summer's kiss,
As did two lovers long ago,
In the first garden God did grow.

Ladybug

A ladybug coloured red
Stayed in my garden til she was fed.
Then spread her wings and flew away.
Please come again my little friend.
You are welcome here on any day.

Building a Fence

The fence was broken.
My neighbour and I had spoken
And I was the one to do the repair.
Should be easy, right? Not a care.
First a post fell on my toes.
Only the beginning of my woes!
The delivery truck was late —
I stewed as I had to wait.
Finally ready to start,
I'd forgotten to take the old fence apart.
Every nail I struck seemed to bend.
My neighbour had forgotten the beer he'd
promised to send.
After many hours of things going wrong,
The fence stood there tall and strong.
My neighbour came for a look
Said he, "It's all crooked like your
line must have been mistook."

Sunflowers

I saw you from afar.
Each flower a giant yellow star
Shining bright above the old brick wall.
I knew then I had to call.
As I made my way down the path,
I just had to laugh,
For you brought me such merriment and joy
As if I were still a boy.
Finally, there you stood —
Tall, stately and good.
Sunflower, I'm glad I came to see you on that day.
My only regret, I did not have longer to stay.

The Artist

For Brenda

The artist sits at her easel
Patiently painting the flowers.
The petunias, the lavender, the teasel.
She can sit there for hours.
Her eyes see something ours never will,
For there is a secret beauty in the garden.
To put it to canvas takes a special skill.

Pixies, Sprites, Trolls and Gnomes

Pixies, sprites, trolls and gnomes,
They make the garden their homes.
Though I've never seen any myself,
They must sneak around with great stealth.
However, there is that time I'd rather forget —
I'd come home from the pub more than a little wet.
There they were, standing at the gate.
"Hurry home," they called, "the
Mrs. says you're late."

Autumn

Red, orange, yellow, brown,
All the leaves are down.
The trees now are bare.
Jack Frost is in the air.
I best go out while I still can,
Or I won't be a happy man.
Soon my hands will be cold, my feet numb,
As autumn sets the table for
the winter yet to come.

Rain

I dislike the rain when I'm out in it,
Whether it be a downpour or just a spit.
But the ground needs rain
To become moist again,
So too do the reservoirs to the north.
In the summer we'll appreciate their worth.
While I may not get along with rain,
I'm always glad to see it back again.

The Weed

There's a weed grows outside my door.
It knows not that it's a weed, or even what for.
Silly human labels confuse things, that's all they do.
For in truth, I am only me, and you are only you.

COWBOYS

Cloudburst

We'd seen the storm coming for hours.
It finally caught us up on the ridge.
We were calling on all of our powers,
Hoping to make it to the bridge.
We were soaked clear through to the bone.
The horses shivered all around.
They clearly wanted to be home
In their stalls, safe and sound.
All of a sudden, the sky opened up.
Gone was the rain, there was the sun.
We all let out a "whoop 'em up!"
As we let the horses run.
Soon we saw smoke rising from the woods ahead.
In the clearing lay that little cabin of pine wood.
At last there was the old homestead.
That old ranch house had
never looked so good.

The Old Rattler

The old rattler suns himself
Down below on a rocky shelf.
I'll leave him to his sunny day,
'Tis time I be on my way.

Mending a Fence

I'm mending a fence out near the wood.
If it keeps my mind from straying, that's good.
Lately I've been thinking too much
About women, and whiskey, memories, and such.
Maybe I just needed some time to be alone,
Out here where the cattle roam.
Out here where it all makes so much sense,
For God's plans were always greater than men's.

The Old Cowboy

The old cowboy spit a chaw in the dust.
"Dag nanit," he said in disgust.
"They turned the meadow into a big box store
Now I can't sit there anymore."

Don't Read My Mind

"Quit tryin' to read my mind.
You ain't likely to like what you're gonna find:
Some cobwebs and dust, a few old girlfriends
and an empty whiskey bottle or two.
So girl, I'm warning you, you
better watch what you do."

Only Friends

The cowboy looked round for a place to sit.
It looked like he'd had a hard day, and was
done with it.
The weather outside was wet and getting wetter.
The beer in his hand would soon make things
feel better.
But the place was a might busy on a Friday
afternoon,
It began to look like he wouldn't be sitting soon.
As he passed by my table, I motioned he should
take a load off his feet.
"Thank you stranger," he said. "Son," I replied,
"There are no strangers here.
Only friends I have yet to meet."

The Last Roundup

I carry a picture of my girl next to my heart.
She's been the one right from the start.
She's waited while I rode this open range,
Though a hundred times I told her I would change.
But the cowboy life had a hold on me,
"What man," I ask, "does not hanker to be
free?"
My love for her, though, is stronger.
It is clear I must wait no longer.
So when this roundup is over, I'll ask her for her
hand.
Together we will build a life in this mighty land.

The Old Truck

The old truck had seen better days.
Now she lay in a field, rusted out, faded by the
sun's rays.
Her hood lay open, all of her tires were flat.
Her seat was gone, where once a driver had sat.
In my mind I could hear her engine roar
out loud.
She must have been so proud.
Weeds grew around her now as if a heavenly
shroud.
I silently paid my respects that day.
Tipped my hat, then I was on my way.

Cowboy Tears

Something splashes in the dust.
Can I lift my head? I must.
Just in time to see her walk on by,
The one that I love on the arm of another guy.
She was mine once, you know.
Until that day she had to go.
Now I spend my days on this old bench.
My love for her I'll never quench.
As for that splashing in the dust, have no fears.
For, if the truth be known, they
are my cowboy tears.

THIS 'N' THAT

The Passion of Summer

Oh to sleep away this rain,
To awake and find it's summer again.
A warm breeze caresses my face.
The garden is perfect, not a plant out of place.
A riot of colour erupts from within,
Inviting me once again to step in,
And feel once more the passion of summer.

My Dreams

I keep my dreams in a box —
A small wooden one high upon a shelf.
I need no key or no locks.
No one would steal them but my self.
And that just wouldn't do,
So there they sit way up high,
Til one day God wills they should come true.
But I tell you now, I won't be shy,
Every single dream I have is one of you.

Don't Quote Me

Most of the quotes I've ever read
Were written by those long since dead.
So I'll not be the one to write a quote,
And settle instead for just a note.

Paris

Oh to be young
And in love
In Paris
In the springtime.
With the cherry blossoms,
And the daffodils.
A hint of rain
In the air,
Other lovers
Walking by.
You look at them
In the eye.
To let them know
You know their secret too.

Progress

The power went out today.
My wife and I sat there with nothing to say.
The computer was down, the T.V. and radio
wouldn't play.
Years ago it must have always been this way,
Until this thing they call progress came along,
Now we're singing a different song.
The voices we had once now are gone.
I get this feeling something
here's gone terribly wrong.

The Poet's Last Request

Once a poet lay dying,
His family at the bedside crying.
"Please," he said to his wife,
"Finish my book. It was my life."
So once the poet had passed,
The old girl went out and got just gassed.
Then she wrote, and she wrote nonstop.
The book sold well, went straight to the top.
One evening, she prayed to God to talk to her feller,
"Hey you old buzzard, "she said,
"we got ourselves a bestseller!"

Never

We put our morning faces on and go out into
the day
Hoping against hope we'll know just what to
do, what to say.
This game called life is never easy to play.
We laugh, we hope, we stumble; trying to find
our way.
The armour we've painted on can only hide so
much,
When often all we need is a kind word, a gentle
smile or loving touch.
Many times I have wondered what I might give
for just the right words to say,
But we all know the rules, how the game must
play.
Never let 'em know, never let it show,
Never let 'em see you crying.

Las Campanas

Yo oigo las campanas,
Las campanas sensillas.
Yo oigo las campanas,
Las campanas de la eglasia,
Las campanas de mi Corazon.

Old Photos

I don't look at old photos anymore.
My life has been a revolving door.
People in my life come and go so fast,
So I'll put those old photo albums away,
And do my best to live just for today.

The Charade

You always said just the right thing
How you could, I was impressed.
I was just a kid, but then you were everything.
I love the way you talked, the way you dressed.
Appearances, though, are often deceiving.
One day I just stopped believing.
For even when it seemed you had it made,
Those sad blue eyes could hide no
longer behind the charade.

The Ol' Rock Wall

That old rock wall now is falling down.
I never thought it would.
In the church yard on the edge of town,
That's where it stood.
But everything one day returns to earth,
So I'll take a photo, for what it's worth.

Dear Mr. Jesus
(My New Shoes)

Dear Mr. Jesus, how are you up there in the sky?
My dad says down here we're just getting by.
Sometimes him and mommy fight,
When they think we're sleeping, late at night.
I don't like it when they're mad at each other.
It's really hard on me and my brother.
I was wondering if there was anything you
could do?
I'm only asking because I trust in You.
Thanks for listening to my prayer.
I'd like to meet you when you come down from
up there.
Until then, I'll be in church on Sunday,
But not Saturday, that's my fun day.
You won't miss me, but if you need any clues,
I'll be the one wearing the new pair of shoes.
Bye for now, your good friend, Billy.
By the way, this week at school
I won't do anything silly.

BRIC A BRAC

Dancing Alone

Have you ever heard the music playing sweet,
soft and low?
It came from somewhere, but you didn't know.
So you asked your sweetie if she'd like to dance.
It was in her eyes, you could see the romance.
You danced and you danced til it was time to
go home.
When the lights came on, you noticed you'd
been dancing alone.
No matter, you thought, better off to dance
Than to never have taken the chance.

The Storms of Winter

As the storm slowly crescendos, I find you with
my arms and pull you into me.
Tender, soft, warm, you ease my fears.
I feared the violent storms as a child,
with their devil-may-care destruction of
anything that was good and nice.
Oh what they did to my favorite trees?
The storms came only in winter then.
Now they seem to come more often.
With you here near me, they seem
much quieter, almost peaceful.

The Keeper of Light

The silence of a falling star
Makes me wonder who you are.
I, who am human, stand in awe of your might,
But I think what moves me most is the power of
your light.
How can you light this planet and maybe even
more?
Have you been here forever or even still before?
The answers to my questions can only come
from you.
So I think I know just what it is that I have to do.
If I said a prayer to you, would you answer me
tonight?
I'd like to get to know you,
The Keeper of the Light.

Tomorrow

If I could hold tomorrow in my hand
To live the life, to do the things I'd planned,
I'm not sure any more what I'd do.
The dreams of yore are gone, they're through.
Life, I've found, is a game of chance.
Some days you cry, some days you dance.
It makes no sense to scheme and plan.
So if I could hold tomorrow in my hand,
I'd simply try to be a better man.

The Face of God

Strange it was this dream I had,
I dreamt of faces, some happy, some sad.
And in every face I did see,
The face of God, looking back at me.

The Nights are Colder

The nights are getting colder.
How I wish that I could hold her
The way I used to not so long ago.
When there would come a chilling snow
There was no heat in our flat,
But we made up for that.
We only had each other to keep warm
As we waited out the winters storm.
Times were much simpler then.
We'd only eat what food our parents could send
I think of those days often now,
And what I would give to go back somehow.

Another Poem About Kissing

Not another poem about kissing!
There always seems to be something missing.
I think I finally figured it out —
Your lips are not the ones they're writing about.
Since your kisses are always the best,
I'll leave it there and disregard the rest.

On Pondering Light

I take for granted light, but it is everywhere.
But it is light that guides me through each day.
Light is in my life in every way —
From the morning sunlight to the bedside lamp
at night.
Everything I do is somehow guided by a light:
There are stoplights, flashlights, and more.
There is a lighted sign in front of every store.
What's more, it is sunlight that warms the earth
and helps the plants make food.
Too much or too little light can alter my mood.
The scientists would tell us it is electromagnetic
radiation,
But that's way beyond my meager education.
So if I call it simply light, I don't care.
I'll just go on being thankful that it's there.

The Poet's Lunch

I had a poet once to lunch.
It was on a whim, just a hunch.
I hoped that he would have something
enlightening for to say,
Instead the droll little man near ruined my day.
All he talked about was himself,
How he was entitled to fame and wealth.
And so another lesson learned,
Not quite so bad as it turned.

Wouldn't You Know It

The man at the publishing house slaps my
poems on the table.
"Well son," he says, "I'd help you if I were able,
"But I've got more poets than I know what to
do with.
"They write about war, they write about love.
"They write about fable, truth and myth."
It seems I'll just have to try again.
So I put on my old grey coat, and step out into
the rain.
Wouldn't you just know it,
Everybody wants to be a poet.

Saint Anthony

I wrote a poem and placed it down
In a spot I thought it would be found.
But much to my great disbelief,
It was stolen by a thief.
I looked and I looked everywhere.
Surely, I thought, this could not be fair.
I'd spent hours on that poem
Only to have it grow legs and roam.
I implored St. Anthony to do his bit,
And in the end my poem was
right there where I'd left it.

Meditation

I once lay me down in a field of grass
To seek the meaning of life.
The clouds looked so peaceful in the sky,
And a breeze blew across my face.
The answers were there within my grasp
When the phone rang.
It was my wife.

DARK NIGHTS AND DEEP WATERS

Is Poetry Passion?

Is poetry passion?
Is passion in fashion?
Has it ever mattered?
My words now are scattered
As leaves in a windstorm.
Happy never to conform.

Today

Today is only yesterday's tomorrow —
A day I truly had to borrow.
So please let me spend my time on you
Until that day the debt becomes due.

The Sins of Today (Redemption Prayer)

God, please let the night wash away the sins of
the day.
Grant me this Lord, and no more will I pray.
It's been three years now that I've carried this gun.
I fear I know not what I've done.
Many are the villages and towns we've plundered,
While overhead the cannons thundered.
The generals in the back urged us on.
"This is just war," they said.
They thought not at all of the blood and tears
that were shed.
If for me there is a tomorrow
I shall spend it bent in sorrow.
No longer can I look in the mirror,
For I have sacrificed everything that I ever
held dear.
Lord, please let this night wash away my sin.

A Field of Stones

In a field of stones I wandered
Contemplating a life half squandered.
The sun was my only friend,
There with me to the end.
Til darkness spread her cloak
And a fire in me awoke
To guide me to my home.
My spirit no longer to roam.

Pills

Six in the morning, seven at night.
Six in the morning, seven at night.
I hope my doctor got the dosage right.
Doctor says to take your pills,
Soon they'll fix all your ills.
If you take them all the right way,
You just might live to see another day,
So you can help the pill makers get richer.
Is there something wrong with this picture?
Blue ones, green ones, yellow ones, pink ones,
All you need is a doctor's note.
Blue ones, green ones, orange ones, red ones,
I feel like I'm pouring a rainbow down my throat.
Six in the morning, seven at night.
Six in the morning, seven at night.

Sheldon

"Hi my name is Sheldon, if you could only get
me to say my name.
I've live here inside my head where every day is
a game.
I look out at you and you look in at me,
But nobody's really certain what it is they see.
The eyes look in, the eyes look out,
You wonder why it is when I shout.
The eyes look in, the eyes look out,
I've been called a fool, a moron and a freak.
There's so much that I could tell you if I could
only speak.
Think I'll go back to my corner, to my rocking chair,
I don't know what the world would do
If they couldn't find me there.

Tequila

Tequila never wrote her a letter.
Tequila never said it was sorry.
Tequila always made him feel better,
Took away every care and every worry.
But it could not meet his every demand,
So he died with a bottle in his hand.
Tequila never did say it was sorry.

Passion

Let not words be the chains that tie you to the
ground.
Let them be instead fiery poetry that sears your
very soul.
I've looked around some and this is what
I've found:
A life without passion is like a
deep and muddy hole.

Two Men

I cannot be two men, you see.
The one I am, and the one you
would have me be.

Blue Sky

Why is the sky blue?
What does it matter to you?
Or is it best left untold?
A silent beauty to behold.

Curse or Verse

I wrote a verse lest I'd forgot
How to put my pen to thought.
There it was, plain to see,
A picture of the man I longed to be.
This need I have to put my pen to verse
I find is often little more than a curse.

She

She died in the winter when the snow was on
the ground.
No one seemed to care, no one said a prayer.
They didn't even want her around,
Just another wayward soul searching for a home.
No longer would she roam.
All the good and righteous folk said it was a
shame she'd ended up this way.
No one said a prayer, no one seemed to care.
There wasn't much more to say,
So they went to the tavern and drank to their
health.
They talked about their families, they talked
about their wealth.
Two days later, they scraped the snow from the
ground and buried her in a pauper's grave.
The preacher said a prayer. No one else was
there.
"Sad," he thought. "We didn't even know her
name.
"No matter, in the eyes of the Lord
we are all one and the same."

Dragons

If you go slaying dragons they won't be hard to
find.
They live in the cracks between night and day,
or in a worried mind.
Dragons are not made of paper, nor wood, nor
flesh, nor bone.
Yet they somehow have a life that's all their own.
When slaying dragons, it seems to me, one
ought to beware,
For who will be the next to
haunt the dragon's lair.

Fire

I lit a fire once to watch it burn.
I failed to see how it all could turn.
For soon the servant became the master.
The flames burned higher, the flames burned
faster,
Until they singed my very soul.
Beware the Devil's mistress for
she's beyond control.

The Photograph

A picture of us came to my attention
By an old friend who just thought he'd mention
How good the two of us looked together.
He said that he wondered whether
We had seen each other lately.
I told him that he had helped me greatly.
Then motioned that he should find the door
While I tore the photo in two
and threw it on the floor.

Octavius

Through the swirling mists of time, a lone rider
came.
"Octavius, Octavius," he called out my name.
"The emperor has decreed you should come
back."
"It's the Goths, they're about to attack."
The very name filled me with dread,
For many would be the dead.
"But I live here now," I said, "Never to return."
"Fine," he replied as he turned his horse,
"They say that Rome will burn."

That Old Tattoo

I finally got rid of that old tattoo.
Do you remember when we got them, me and you?
It was so long ago now I can hardly remember.
Five years I believe come this September.
Our love was new then, and full of promise.
Everyone said that we just couldn't miss.
But people, like the weather, often change,
As their lives they try to rearrange.
One day the words, "Julie I love you forever,"
Just didn't have the magic anymore.
I'm so glad now I had it removed,
But man, is my arm sore.

Love by Moonlight

Love by moonlight
I find is quite alright.
No sun to blind my eyes
As I tear at your disguise
To find the treasure hidden there.
With the moon our love we'll share.

Critics

We knew not how it would go
When we set out to see the show.
The critics had given it bad reviews.
Never mind them, the critics are bad news.
To be truly entertained, one must often take a
chance.
It was quite a show about song and dance.
We found it to be really quite good.
If you were thinking of seeing it, you should.
And to all you critics — Ahem!!
If you knew about movies,
you'd be making them.

The Empty Vase

The empty vase sits on a table.
I'd put flowers there if I were able.
To will these legs to walk out that door,
To skip, to run, to dance like once before.

Turquoise and Silver

Turquoise and silver was the bracelet
That she was wearing when they first met.
She said she'd found it somewhere in the
southwest,
The artisans there, she said, were the best.
Her wrists were long and slender.
He thought of the roses he would send her.
Only one problem did remain,
He didn't yet know her name.

Moments in Time

Your eyes, your smile, your face.
Some other time, some other place.
Your memory drifts back to me slow,
It was such a long time ago.
We were lovers in ancient Rome.
You a noblewoman, I a minstrel without a home.
How we met, I do not recall.
For a moment, didn't we have it all?
Long afternoons spent in bed.
Quiet times, nothing said.
I could have frozen those moments in time.
Alas, the decision was never mine.
Father Time plays favourites to no one.
One day our love was simply done.
I never saw you again, until now.
Though many times I thought we'd meet
somehow.
Why did we finally meet today?
Is there yet to be a final act to our play?

Cancion De Me Corazon

La cancion de mi corazon
No tiene parablas.
Pera la musica es hermosa
Al iqual que los olas en la playa.

Stars

If you've never seen the stars from the gutter,
You've never seen the stars at all.
Preposterous, I know, you should utter,
But how can we see the truth if we never fall?

Lifeblood

A river runs by my door
A thousand miles or maybe more.
It starts in the mountains far away.
The water flows but it can never stay.
For it is the lifeblood of this land,
It's nurturing moisture in high demand.
Through the valleys, forests and towns it goes,
Past the factories, the farms, the thirsty cities it
flows.
And finally on down to the sea,
The river rolls on to eternity.

Empires of Sand

Castles we built on the beaches' summer sands,
Every detail sculpted with loving hands.
Then the battles that we fought
With the starfish and the crabs that we'd caught.
There were no winners or losers in this game.
The tide washed everything clean all the same.
Perhaps one day we'd come to understand
What fate held for empires built on sand.

The Hawk and the Crow

A death in the afternoon.
Some would say it came too soon.
The crow was a yearling barely out the nest
When in one fell swoop, the hawk laid its soul
to rest.
I thought for a moment as I sat in a pause,
It is sad but nature has its own set of laws.

HAIKU

24 Haiku Poems

Winter Wren's song,
From my garden like a poem,
Tells me I am not alone.

Soft pink cherry blossoms
Blessing my garden briefly.
Soon to blow away.

Sunlight brightens day.
Soon sun sets til tomorrow.
Nothing stays the same.

Rain on my window
Wakes me from a summer dream.
Leaves blow in the breeze.

A candle burns bright,
Brings light to a darkened room,
As you light my life.

A match burns so bright,
Soon lost amongst starry night.
Quickly flickers, fades.

Your ocean blue eyes
Call to me to swim inside
And we will be one.

For a mother.
You who were everything
And I couldn't say goodbye.

Papa do you hear?
My voice is so loud and clear.
Did we ever talk?

Old man looks at life
Like sand slipped through fingers.
Not wasted, only gone.

A small ginger cat,
Like his cousin the lion,
Stalks prey in my yard.

Soft pink perfection,
You come to me in spring.
How I await you.

In a lonely room
Guitar hangs on empty wall.
No one to play her.

Why are we old now?
We were younger when we met.
Do you like it here?

I hear the silence...
...of the sounds of the city.
They all blend to one.

Your hair was as gold.
The flowers I recall blue.
They matched so well.

The grass grows higher.
Sadly, I grow lazier.
How long can I sit?

Often in my dreams
My ancestors hunt bison.
So long ago now.

Black dog is my friend.
When no others spoke with me,
His friendship was there.

Summer rain I ask,
Could you wash my body clean?
Renew my newness.

Old book sits on shelf
With so much knowledge to share,
Yet no one reads you.

Once a paradise...
Now forests gone, sea's empty.
The fool soils his bed.

Kingfisher awaits.
Time spent on that lonely wire
May yet yield a fish.

Crow tells a story
From high up in the pine tree.
He cares not who hears.

Haiku Trio

Come in the gate, friend.
I will show you my garden.
Beauty I must share.

The peaceful teahouse.
No harsh words are spoken here.
Drink in the beauty.

Walk with me, my friend,
For my garden knows no end.
So too, our friendship.

Walking Tanka

He dreamt of walking.
The dream was always out there.
Just a simple dream
Calling him to walk again.
In his heart he knew he would.

Printed in Canada